Get Set For Fun

Written by David Lavelle

Collins

Get set! Put on boots.

Pack a map in a rucksack.

Go up a hill. Go back down!

Go up a ladder.

Run in the rain.

Look for earwigs in the moss.

Dip for fish in rock pools.

Set up a den at sunset.

Hear owls hoot in the dark.

See bats zip by.

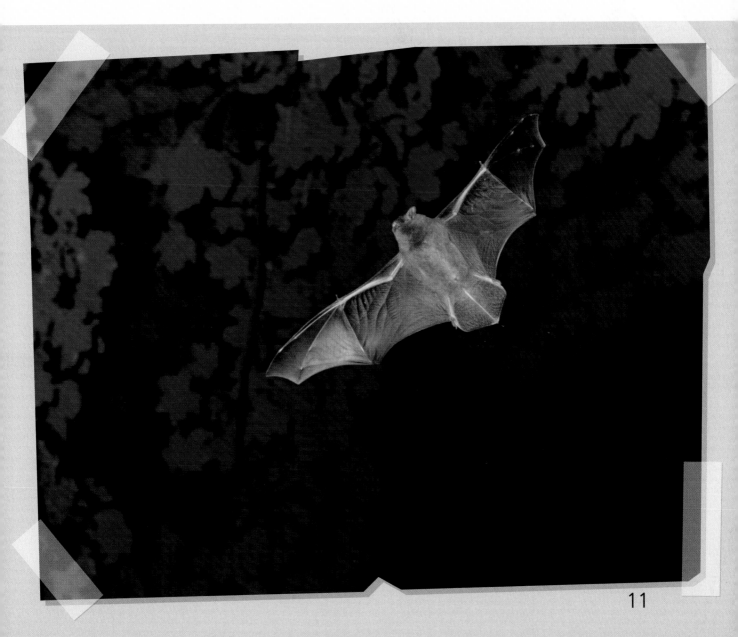

Cook food at night.

See the moon.

Get set
boots ✓
map ✓

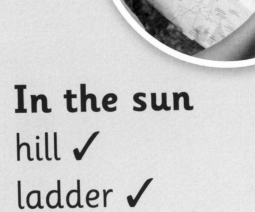

In the sun
hill ✓
ladder ✓

In the wet
rain ✓
earwigs ✓
rock pools ✓

At night
den ✓
food ✓
moon ✓

 Review: After reading

Use your assessment from hearing the children read to choose any GPCs, words or tricky words that need additional practice.

Read 1: Decoding

- Practise reading multi-syllable words together. Look at the word **rucksack** together. Ask the children to sound talk and blend the letter sounds in each syllable "chunk": ruck/sack
- Do the same with the following words:

  sun/set

  ear/wigs

Read 2: Prosody

- Choose two double page spreads and model reading with expression to the children. Ask the children to have a go at reading the same pages with expression.
- Reread the whole book to the children to model fluency and rhythm in the story.

Read 3: Comprehension

- Look at pages 14 and 15 together. Talk about the activities the children did in the book, such as when they were getting ready (get set), in the sun, in the rain and in the dark.
- For every question ask the children how they know the answer. Ask:
  - What nighttime animals did you see in the book? (*owl*, *bat*)
  - Which of the activities in the pictures would you most like to do? Why?